PRACTICE MAKES PERMANENT

WHAT WARRIORS TEACH US
ABOUT CHARACTER,
LEADERSHIP, AND TRUST

ANTHONY RANDALL

FREILING
PUBLISHING

Published by Freiling Publishing,
a division of Freiling Agency, LLC.
P.O. Box 1264
Warrenton, VA 20188

www.FreilingPublishing.com

Paperback ISBN: 978-1-956267-36-5
eBook ISBN: 978-1-956267-37-2

Printed in the United States of America

*To my amazing wife and children and to
those I have the privilege to serve alongside.
Show Up. Play Up. Finish.*

ENDORSEMENTS

"If you are wondering how we might emerge stronger from the crises and conflicts of recent years, read this book. But do more than that. Practice does make permanent. Anthony Randall explains how we can work together to strengthen our families, communities, and our nation to build a better future for generations to come."

–H. R. McMaster, author,
Battlegrounds and *Dereliction of Duty*.

"High-performing leaders in high stakes situations will find this book valuable. Anthony Randall draws from his remarkable life to produce straightforward insights and solid advice for leaders who are guiding their followers to become better versions of themselves. I especially appreciate his unique ability to merge practical, gritty insights into the elegant framework of Aristotle's approach to rhetoric, politics, and ethics."

–Dr. Robert M. Franklin, President Emeritus, Morehouse College. Laney Professor in Moral Leadership, Emory University

"Every teacher hopes one day his students will do something or be someone better than the teacher. My student Anthony Randall makes a valuable moral statement far better than any I've ever made. Read it and grow!"

–Dr. Nate Zinsser, author, *The Confident Mind*, Director, Performance Psychology Program, USMA

"I've known Anthony for a long time. I know the men and the stories he shares in detail. His experience spans from the board room to the battlefield, from professional sports to the profession of arms. He is part of a rare breed that can blend rigorous academic study with application in the real world. His ability to blend high-level concepts and convert them into practice is enviable. I encourage you to read and practice these concepts as a permanent part of your leadership and life."

–JEFF TIEGS (LTC, Ret.), US Army Special Forces

"Practice is the only path towards permanent change." Since meeting him after being drafted by the Pittsburgh Pirates in 2011, Anthony Randall has been the epitome of character and leadership. Ten years later, I'm able to call myself not only a big-leaguer and an all-star but also a man of character and a man of God. This book embodies some of the keys that helped shape our culture and my journey from the minor leagues to the majors."

–JOSH BELL, First Basemen, Washington Nationals, 2019 MLB All-Star & Home Run Derby

"I connected with the book, *Practice Makes Permanent*. It explores the principles I used to defy the odds and accomplish my dreams."

–DAVID ECKSTEIN, 2x World Series Champion, 2006 World Series MVP

"The lessons in Anthony's book remind us that a life well-lived requires traits like commitment and character. My 28 years of military service taught me that your character is your currency. Whether serving in combat, leading organizational change, or completing Ranger School, I rely on the same attribute based principles Anthony lays out to complete my mission."

–WALT ZAJKOWSKI, Command Sergeant Major, US Army, 2X Best Ranger Competition Winner

"There is one-way true leadership is manifest—and that is through a wholly integrated life, committed to intimate relationships and performance excellence. As the Commander of Fort Benning for two years, working alongside Anthony, I watched him live this out every single day. His life—with his family, peers, subordinates, and superiors—constantly demonstrates the "permanence" of "practice." This book not only reflects truth; it also is an accurate testament to Anthony's understanding, internalization, and manifestation of real leadership."

–LIEUTENANT GENERAL ERIC J. WESLEY, (USA, Retired)

"*Practice Makes Permanent* breaks the bell curve of leadership book mediocrity. Anthony Randall's direct application of the warrior culture and hard lessons learned will enable readers to build their own foundation for moral leadership. Randall cleanly lays out a path delineated by virtues and provides examples in practice, bookended with actionable takeaways. This quick read provides reminders architected to help readers avoid falling victim to their own vanity, denials, and rationalizations, which can be extended to an entire organization. Randall imbues this work with a spirit of internally fueled self-obedience that ultimately enables the conquest of self-doubt and instability, resulting in a confident leadership model with a definitive organizational halo effect."

–WHITFIELD ATHEY, CFO, Delta Data,
Mutual Fund Thought Leader

"Most of us in positions of leadership or influence know the problem, my friend Anthony Randall states it succinctly, "We have a leadership crisis of character necessitating a call to action." Anthony provides solid solutions of applicable wisdom gained from real world experience. It will no doubt be one of my few highly recommended books for those who feel called or drawn to any level of leadership."

–VICTOR MARX, President & CEO
All Things Possible Ministries

"As a man of faith, character, and integrity, my friend Anthony Randall has written a book that moves us from solid information to practical action! Through vivid stories, research, and experience, "Practice Makes Permanent" can help us all understand the true importance of practice so we can improve as leaders and as people. If you are looking for substance, depth, and a proven roadmap for growth - written by someone who has been on the front lines, does the hard work, and continues to courageously and vulnerably enter the arena—this is your book."

–STEVE SHENBAUM, Founder &
President of Game On Nation

"You've got two choices on how you respond to this book. One is to discard the message because you think Anthony is bragging about his life achievements. He's not; he's merely backing up his call to excellence by documenting his own commitment to practice it. The other choice is to heed and obey that calling in you that resonates with Anthony's challenge. I hope this is the choice you make. You, your family, our country, our world is counting on your choosing this path."

–REGGIE MCNEAL, leadership coach and best-selling author *Practicing Greatness, A Work of Heart*

CONTENTS

INTRODUCTION

THERE IS A crisis of leadership in our country, in our communities, in our churches, in our corporations, and within ourselves. Throughout history, people have sought to resolve crises through epistemological, ethical, logical, and metaphysical studies. Others, people like myself, value these studies through the lens of a different ethos—the ethos of a martial artist and professional soldier. One of the most important professions of human flourishing that is critical to the moral, ethical, and just conduct of any tribe or nation state is that of the warrior profession. This is my ethos.

What is our crisis?

Our nation's civic public square that was founded upon the virtues of classic liberalism and republicanism is being destroyed by the vices of religious totalitarianism and progressive secularism. Educated derelicts, bully pulpits, and a society overloaded with information yet lacking process and pragmatic application is intended to blunt moral courage, baffle the clear mind, and burden the soul. We are being numbed into mediocrity.

What shall we do about it?

We have a leadership crisis of character necessitating a call to action. We must teach and train moral agents of character to lead as trusted professionals. We must reclaim the civility of the public square with virtuous intent, critical thinking, and courageous action. Practitioners of virtuous character and lifelong pursuers of living a more excellent way must reclaim the civility of the public square with professional discourse and transformational practice.

Aristotle, one of several ancient writers who influenced Western philosophical thought, promoted a lifestyle of practice pursuing excellence. Roman stoicism followed suit. The Jewish historian, Josephus, portrayed this image of pursuing excellence and how practice makes permanent when he wrote of the Roman Army's training methodology in his book, *A History of the Jewish War*:

> If you study, carefully the organization of the Roman Army, you will realize that they possess a great empire as a reward for valor, not as a gift of fortune. For the Romans, the wielding of arms does not begin with the outbreak of

war, nor do they sit idly by in peacetime, or only move their hands during times of need—quite the opposite! As if born for the sole purpose of wielding arms, they never take a break from training, never wait for a situation requiring arms. Their practice sessions are no less strenuous than real battles. Each soldier trains every day with all his energy as if in war. Therefore, they bear the stress of battle with the greatest of ease. No confusion causes them to break from their accustomed formation, no fear causes them to shrink back, no exertion tires them. Certain victory always attends them since their opponents are never equal to them. So, you could call their practice sessions bloodless battles and their battles bloody practice sessions.[1]

Sensei Masutatsu Oyama said it this way, "If someone asked me what a human being ought to devote the maximum of his life to, I would answer: training. Train more than you sleep."[2]

I spent over 20 years as a professional soldier and 30 years as a martial artist, studying and training in the art and science of praxis, pursuing excellence, and preparing for the battles of life, spiritually, mentally, and physically. This is what I've learned—practice *does not* make perfect; practice makes *permanent…so practice with passion, purpose, and precision.*

Let me repeat that—practice makes permanent. Today, I teach, train, and coach transformational moral leadership. The methodology consists of virtue ethics, moral reasoning, ethical decision making, and emotionally intelligent leadership. Such a deontological approach aims to achieve the telos, or end state, of mitigating immoral, unethical behavior and assessing and selecting trusted leaders of character who shape culture and influence climates of high-performing organizations.

This book will help you build high-performing cultures around leaders of character. You can build high-performance cultures around leaders of character OR you can enable characters to destroy your high-performing culture. Leaders of character leverage the crisis-solving ethos I've learned and teach. The way of the warrior is your path to finally solving the crises in your life and in the life of the organization you lead.

I invite you to join me in a four-book series investigating how practice makes permanent. A holistic approach to character development requires the three pillars of transformational moral leadership—moral courage, moral reasoning, and moral empathy. I believe transformational moral leadership elevates, expands, refines, and forges people of excellence through moral courage, moral reasoning, and moral empathy.

In this book, *Practice Makes Permanent*, we will address how high-character individuals and high-performance cultures practice breaking the bell curve of mediocrity while pursuing the mean of Aristotle's excellence, or *eudaimonia*. We will observe how leaders of character practice showing up, playing up, and finishing. We will practice being purposeful in the present. We will be precise in aiming for what's next. Practice does make permanent, so make sure what you practice is perfect.

In my next book, *Ethos: Practicing Who You Are*, we will address the essence of teaching and training transformational leaders of trusted character established upon moral courage. Plato argues that courage is the enduring virtue of the soldier. Geoffrey Scarre writes, "Moral courage is the greatest virtue a transformational moral leader must possess. It leads to effective implementation and practice of other associated virtues such as charity, justice, wisdom, and patience."[3]

Winston Churchill opined from Aristotle's original thought that when speaking of human qualities, courage should be the first mentioned. Churchill believed courage an essential virtue that enable all others. In the Aristolean tradition of seeking the golden mean by avoiding the vices of excess and deficiency, moral courage is located between emotivism of fear and actions of bravado and recklessness. Aristotle writes, "It [moral virtue] is a state of character, not a passion, nor a capacity."

Complex environments require leaders with moral character founded in moral courage, not emotivism. Moral courage is a non-negotiable bedrock for transformational moral leaders, establishing a foundation for right intent, right action, and hopefully, right result. The warrior ethos will represent a model for practicing an ethos answering, "Who are you as a trusted leader of character?"

Then in my third book, *Logos: Practicing How You Make Decisions*, we will address how moral reasoning assumes we received free choice and moral autonomy when created in the *imago Dei*, the image of God. As God's creation, people are delineated as separate and what God called "very good" (Genesis 1:31) on the culmination of creation on the day He created man. Therefore, our moral norms and values developed through our moral psychological development determine how we choose to transform or conform. Moral reasoning reveals our decision-making process and what we see as right and just and how we effectively or ineffectively exert our leadership philosophy and styles of leadership. Our moral norms and values collide, conform, or collaborate with our world's heteronymous ethical codes, norms, and values. They provide each of us a greater identity when we join a collective tribe and further shape our identities, decision-making processes, and worldviews. We will investigate the psychological moral development of leaders and decision makers, the pitfalls of moral and ethical failure, and how to implement a high-character, high-performance team of moral and ethical decision makers.

Finally, in my fourth book, *Pathos: Practicing How You Lead*, we will address moral empathy as synonymous with emotional intelligence. Leadership coaching is an essential tool in connecting with leaders to elevate, expand, refine, and forge leaders' abilities to achieve excellence.

Leadership requires connecting, engaging, understanding, and learning from holistic experiences. Leadership requires art, science, cognition, and emotion. Moral empathy shapes the emotionally intelligent leader whose identity and character are reflected in his or her decision-making process, self-awareness, self-management, social awareness, and positive influence in managing relationships.

Transformational moral leadership is the metaphysical, cognitive, and psychological process of moral and ethical leader development. We will establish a foundation, framework, and process for implementing leadership coaching and descriptive learning. Transformational leaders will practice how they lead with six varying styles of emotional intelligence and establish a leadership coaching philosophy. Finally, we will investigate how transformational leaders influence leaders of influence as trusted advisors and trusted agents.

But today, as you hold this book in your hands, I want to introduce you to the warrior way and show you how practice makes permanent. Together, we'll discover how to make lasting and permanent change in your life and in the lives of everyone you touch.

I wrote my first leadership book with a small publishing company in 2002 at 28 years old. Today, it sells on eBay for more than I sold it for in 2002. It is usually accompanied by a caption, "Like New. Perfect Binder. Never opened. Signed by Author." I still have copies in my attic.

On the surface, that may sound like failure. Now, however, after spending 25 years practicing, serving, and leading in high-performance organizations, it is a profound statement to the art of practice. I am a lifelong practitioner of the art and science of leadership.

I want to share with you the most important principles I have practiced, learned, and am still learning. First, practice makes permanent, so make sure what you practice is passionate, purposeful, and precise. The next three principles are integrally related—practicing who you are as a trusted agent of character, practicing how you make moral and ethical decisions, and practicing how you lead yourself, people, and organizations with emotional intelligence.

How have I learned these principles? I've never stopped practicing, even when people and circumstances threatened my practice.

I was a third alternate to attend the United States Military Academy at West Point. The recruiter told me I was "not qualified," yet I graduated on the Dean's List and won a national collegiate championship in my sport. I've been physically assaulted and injured by multiple assailants, publicly slandered, and ostracized for standing my ground as a leader of character. Yet today, my character has led me to serve with some of the most high-performance professionals in the world. I recycled two of the three phases of the U.S. Army Ranger School and graduated the 62-day course in 120 days, yet I later served as cadre at the U.S. Army Ranger School and wrote it's mental conditioning program. I never scored above a combined 1000 on my SATs for college, I failed to finish my GRE in time, yet I earned a 3.0, 3.8, and 4.0 in two master's and one doctorate degree. Through it all, I never stopped practicing.

I have assessed, selected, served, and led in the U.S. military's most elite Special Operations units. I have developed holistic health, resiliency, and ethical leadership programs for elite organizations. I have provided leadership coaching and development to multi-year Major League Baseball playoff teams and provided leadership development for NCAA D1 national championship and runner-up teams. I have served multiple combat tours as an Army Ranger and Army Chaplain, providing spiritual, moral, and ethical counsel, instruction, and leadership to soldiers and senior military leaders in the most adverse conditions. I have planted, pastored, and spiritually led church congregations for over 18 years, walking through the joy and sorrows of life with thousands of parishioners. I am a husband, father, brother, and son still practicing how to achieve excellence in serving those I love.

Today, I own a successful leadership development and executive coaching company working with high-performance leaders and organizations all over the world. I practice the art and science of leadership every day. May I invite you to join me in practice?

PRACTICE MAKES ~~PERFECT~~
PERMANENT

*"Upon the fields of friendly strife are sown
the seeds that, upon other fields, on other
days, will bear the fruits of victory."*
–General Douglas MacArthur

FIELDS OF FRIENDLY STRIFE

AS AN ATHLETE and trainer of athletes, I've learned the importance of practice. For the successful athlete, it's not optional. It's absolutely imperative. Let me explain.

I love baseball. I played through my freshman year of high school. I was cut my sophomore year, but I never stopped studying the game. I've spent several years as a Little League and middle school baseball coach. I was fortunate to spend eight years in Major League Baseball as a leadership coach and chaplain with the Pittsburgh Pirates, including their three-year playoff run from 2013–2015. Baseball fans would argue it is the greatest game ever played. And those who have been in the game, especially the ones at the college and professional levels who have embraced the grind of the game, will tell you this, "Baseball will figure you out before you figure out baseball."

Last fall, I was coaching my youngest son's Little League baseball team in our league playoffs. For fall ball, typically a developmental league season, there was a definite competitiveness in the air. COVID had canceled the spring season, and the fall season seemed to inherit the same energy and hype as a result. So, there we were, up one run in the final inning of a 10-year-old Little League playoff game. Our ace pitcher was pitching exceptionally well, but he started showing fatigue and was near his pitch count limit. I could have kept him in, but I pulled him based upon intuition and experience. At this point of the game, I did what I had done all season. I brought in my closer. It happened to be my son who had racked up four dozen strikeouts that fall and won several games for us. No brainer. No question. Game over, but…we lost.

He gave up several hits, walks, runs, and then more tears on the way home. He went to bed.

I turned on Game 6 of the 2020 World Series. It was a must-win game for the Tampa Bay Rays against the Los Angeles Dodgers. I had an eerie feeling as I tuned in mid-game. Tampa's manager, Kevin Cash, went to his ace, Blake Snell, who had won Game 2. Up one run late in the game, Cash pulled Snell, who was pitching a solid game, and put in the hottest closer in baseball, Nick Anderson, who had a .55 ERA and .49 WHIP. In baseball language, he was virtually unhittable.

No brainer. No question. Game over, but…they lost… the World Series.

This spring, my son returned to the mound in good form, racking up dozens of strikeouts and limiting hits and runners on base. He's only 10. He has years of practice ahead of him if he wants to pursue pitching at the next level. His practice will facilitate permanence of a mental game, arm, body mechanics, and pitching style. He has yet to throw a perfect pitch.

Nick Anderson began the 2021 season rehabbing a partially torn elbow ligament, a potential career-ending injury for a pitcher. This season he's in Triple-A. Having spent eight seasons in minor and major league clubhouses with some of the most high-performance athletes in the world, I can only imagine his daily mental and physical preparation as he steadily increased his fastball over 94 miles per hour, anticipating a call from Kevin Cash back up to "The Show." Nick has likely yet to throw a perfect pitch—the perfect pitch that may even win a World Series.

Athletic competition teaches athletes, coaches, and even observers lifelong lessons. It's why Josephus noted that the Roman legion's intent, action, and end state of practicing sessions of bloodless battles was to ensure their battles were bloody practice sessions. Athletics were utilized by the Greeks and Romans to simulate the thrill of victory and agony of defeat without killing their comrades-in-arms. In martial arts, thousands of hours are spent in the dojo mastering technique, feel, and knowing yourself and your opponent without killing each other. Coaches and athletes learn in the clubhouse and dojo that character and culture are essential to victory on the field of play and, for some, on the field of battle.

On the field of play, decisions have consequences. Every situation is different, calling on leaders to assess their situation and environment accordingly. However, high- performance leaders who are people of character—demonstrating integrity or wholeness in intent, thought, and action—are far more prepared to make the right decision at the right time and with the right intent, due to practice and trusting the process.

Those in the arena are held to a higher standard by the fans in the stands. Most of the fans could never compete at the level of performance demanded by the players. In sports, there is always next season. In other arenas, the essential virtues of a leader's char-acter driving the art and science of practice in their profession leave permanent results—sometimes, life and death.

My point is that through the perseverance of practice, you cannot reach the pinnacle you're aiming for. You want perfection, but what you really need is perma-nence—permanent change that will take you to a higher level. For both my son and MLB players, win or lose, the art of practice never ends. Practice is the only path toward permanent change. Today, our culture looks for shortcuts and short-term solutions to lifelong challenges. The way of the warrior is the opposite. We train and practice for the long term. It's the only way toward transformational leadership.

UPON OTHER FIELDS

THERE'S ANOTHER FIELD, a field I've always played on, where practice is essential. It's where warriors train and fight, win, and yes, sometimes lose battles. Yet the training goes on.

The United States' 20-year anniversary of the Global War on Terror looms large as I write this only a couple of days before the world remembers 9/11. On September 10th, I will attend the retirement ceremony of one of my West Point classmates who was a key leader in the Global War on Terror. On September 11th, I will spend my morning at the U.S. Army's Airborne and Special Operations Museum with a Gold Star Spouse and her family. I was honored to serve with her husband who was killed in Afghanistan. There remains a broad spectrum of political persuasion and personal and professional opinions regarding the start, prolongation, and conclusion of the War on Terror in Afghanistan and Iraq.

Fresh in the minds of American and Afghan citizens and citizens of Allied nations remembering 9/11 is the ill-prepared, ill-planned, and humiliating withdrawal from Afghanistan by the Biden administration. Potentially the greatest foreign policy blunder in the history of the United States exposed American political leaders and their appointees' deficient practices of foreign diplomacy and implementation of Clauswitz's theory of war as an extension of politics.

It highlighted their intellectual *elitism*, arrogance, and subsequent resistance to *elite* professionals, humble servants, and expert practitioners of war such as senior leaders in the military and intelligence community who advised differently. There is a great chasm between "elitists" and those who are "elite." One is achieved by entitlement and the other by practice.

In Richie Norton's book, *The Power of Something Stupid*, Norton shares Stephen Covey's counsel to him when coaching senior leaders, "Covey taught me a priceless principle that would forever change my outlook on the nature of education and experience. He said, 'Richie, experience is overrated. Some people say they have twenty years experience, when, in reality, they only have one year's experience, repeated twenty times.'"[4]

The Afghanistan exit seems to highlight this fact from the top tier of our political establishment. Lieutenant General H.R. McMaster's book, *Battlegrounds,* highlights this point in his prophetic and all-too-revealing chapter titled "A One-Year War Twenty Times Over: America's South Asian Fantasy." He writes that some officials in Washington had "convinced themselves" wrongly that the Taliban was a "benign organization," leading to the usual "strategic narcissism" policy makers succumb to in order to create the enemy they want to engage, rather than the actual enemy they face.[5]

In contrast, what is known about the key leaders who commanded the soldiers, sailors, and airmen and led the historically largest airlift evacuation of over 118,000 people in 14 days out of Kabul International Airport in August 2021? They are elite in their practice; they are excellent in their execution. They are trusted leaders of character.

One key leader in command at Hamid Karzai International Airport was Major General Chris Donahue. Today, he commands the 82nd Airborne Division. He began his career as a professional Army officer on the fields of friendly strife and as an Army football player at West Point. In a highly decorated career as an Army Ranger and infantry officer, he successfully commanded some of the most elite and well-trained military units in the world. He has come face to face with the enemy hundreds of times at the tactical level and defeated them at the operational and strategic level.

His character as a high-performance leader who knows practice makes permanent models a different perspective of leadership. He is a soldier's soldier. He has accomplished any task he might assign his subordinates. He empowers and encourages his team to lead, make decisions, and execute. He collaborates effectively with his peers. He influences senior leaders with empirical and pragmatic wisdom. Most importantly, he has devout convictions about the value of human life, care for soldiers and families, and duty to God and country.

As a leader of character pursuing excellence, he has 30 years of practicing real-world leadership—growing, adapting, and leading organizations—and solving complex problem sets with overwhelmingly successful results. He has been promoted through a meritocracy that awards passionate, purposeful, and precise practice—not personality, popularity, and public opinion. There are very few general officers in our ranks today who could have rapidly planned, coordinated, and conducted the largest humanitarian airlift rescue mission in history while being surrounded by the enemy and successfully evacuated so many people in such dire circumstances. However, he would give all the credit to his team on the ground in Kabul.

I know. I had the privilege of serving with "CD" in combat and in an institutional environment where we trained future military leaders of character. We both find Aristotle's work, *Nicomachean Ethics*, a guide for practicing a life of excellence. It is no mistake that Aristotle's epic work on ethics and living a life of virtue was written and named for his father and son, both named Nichomachus. It is a treatise of living a legacy and pursuing a more excellent life. Aristotle wrote:

> For in everything it is no easy task to find the middle, e.g., to find the middle of a circle is not

for everyone but for him who knows; so, too, anyone can get angry—that is easy—or give or spend money; but to do this to the right person, to the right extent, at the right time, with the right motive, and in the right way, that is not for everyone, nor is it easy; wherefore goodness is both rare and laudable and noble.[6]

Aristotle's mean was not one of mediocrity or the "bell curve." Aristotle's mean is a pursuit of virtue over vice. It exemplifies pursuing a life of excellent practice. A master practitioner with years of excellent practice perfecting training made a world of difference on the Kabul runway in August 2021. Excellence requires an unyielding, unflinching, and uncompromising commitment to practicing, training trust, trusting process, and living out an ethos. It requires breaking the bell curve of mediocrity and pursuing the hard routine of training your trust and trusting your training.

2

BREAKING THE BELL CURVE
OF MEDIOCRITY

"If you know your enemy and know yourself,
you need not fear the result of a thousand battles.
If you know yourself but not the enemy, for every
victory gained, you will also suffer defeat."

–Sun Tzu, *The Art of War*

SUN TZU REMINDS us to know our enemy as well as ourselves. When we choose to live a life of excellence, we must be aware that the greatest enemy may be ourselves. A life of excellence is not defined by or compared to how others around us live or what shifting systematic constructs or cultural norms deem as normal. Those can be subjective and constantly moving goalposts. Practicing a life of excellence by pursuing permanence with passionate, purposeful, and precise practice must rely on ethos, truth, and virtue.

The Apostle Paul, one of the greatest Christian apostles who wrote the majority of the New Testament, refused to compare himself to other religious leaders of the day. Amid their pride, he chose humility. He wrote, "For we dare not class ourselves or compare ourselves with those who commend themselves. But they, measuring themselves by themselves, and not comparing themselves among themselves, are not wise" (2 Corinthians 10:12).

When we simply compare ourselves with others, we become consumed with the bell curve of mediocrity. Our intent is questionable, our thinking benign, our practice mediocre, and our outcomes unpredictable. Breaking the bell curve of mediocrity requires a different perspective.

PURSUING EXCELLENCE WITH CHARACTER
BREAKS THE BELL CURVE OF MEDIOCRITY

HAVE YOU EVER considered that the classic bell curve is a pathway to mediocrity? Think about it. What happened to hiring people of character, developing high-performing cultures, and managing high-capital and high-potential climates? Average organizations, mediocre marketplaces, and middle-of-the-pack teams have capitulated to the bell curve of mediocrity somewhere along the way, accepting the status quo as good enough. The COVID pandemic and Volatile, Uncertain, Chaotic, and Ambiguous (VUCA) environments have exacerbated this phenomenon.

It is typically easy to select out the bottom 20 percent of human capital. They typically select out themselves. The college application is too long. The certification pipeline is too arduous. The standards and expectations are too high. The routine is too hard.

What is left is the mediocre middle. Due to demand for skills, experience, deadlines, job security, and maintaining the status quo, mediocre organizations settle for the mediocre middle. They settle for human capability versus character and potential.

How do high-performing organizations select the top 20 percent of human capital and human potential? From my experience in military Special Operations, college and professional sports, and the corporate world, high-performing organizations prioritize trusted character agents and trusted development processes that elevate and expand human capital and refine and forge human potential with excellence.

One example occurred several years ago while I was serving in the U.S. Army's Airborne and Ranger Training Brigade. My brigade commander was hosting one of the Army's most senior commanders. The commander was keenly interested in the decision-making process of implementing a major paradigm shift in a closely protected warrior ethos—successfully integrating women into the U.S. Army Ranger School, "the Army's toughest course and the premier small unit tactics and leadership school."

The mental, physical, and emotional duress of the 62-day course teaches students tactics and leadership skills necessary to engage with and defeat an enemy in close combat. Ranger School is a leadership school. It assesses an individual's character to lead self, peers, and teams under adversity and duress. As posted at the entrance to Camp Rogers, Ranger School is "Not for the Weak or Faint Hearted." Herein lay the problem. Ranger School was a male-only military school. Would the standards have to change if women were allowed to attend?

Policy makers in Washington, D.C., questioned the funding of a leadership school with a graduation rate that was historically less than 50 percent per class. At the time, some classes dipped into the high 30 percent to low 40 percent range. How was the Army's premier combat leadership school supposed to integrate women? Why should taxpayers and policy makers fund a program that would be considered a failure in any other school?

The room grew quiet with all eyes on my commander, a career Army Ranger, a trusted professional, a man of character, and a high-EQ leader. But before I tell you what he said, consider this.

Traditionally, Ranger School was open only to combat arms soldiers such as infantry, armor, artillery, and some close combat support branches, along with other service branches. However, in April 2011, the Army chose to allow any MOS (Military Occupational Specialty) soldier to attend Ranger School. This coincided with the closing of Army units' Pre-Ranger Courses (PRCs). These courses, conducted at combatant commands such as the 82nd Airborne Division, were shut down due to funding and manpower shortages attributed to the wars in Iraq and Afghanistan. Historically, combatant commands conducted PRCs to initially assess and select personnel who could demonstrate the character traits and basic technical skills necessary to attend the Ranger Course and potentially graduate.

Enter the bell curve of mediocrity. The Army enlarged the pipeline with the number of personnel available to attend the Ranger Course through transactional management of enabling any MOS to attend while subsequently removing the transformational leadership PRCs capable of assessing and selecting qualified candidates.

The bell curve of mediocrity promotes fairness over equality and quantity over quality. Organizations and organizational leaders who pursue excellence seek out leaders of character with the capital and potential to succeed while gaining skills and experience in the process. They reject mediocrity and look for candidates who excel by character through their acquiring, training, and transition process of empowering human capital and potential. Invariably, a higher standard increases quality-of-character candidates while providing equal opportunity for anyone to demonstrate character, capital, and potential for excellence.

Back to the hush-toned room with all eyes on my commander. He paused, collected his thoughts, and with the utmost excellence of a trusted professional, candidly and respectfully expressed to the senior Army leader that the character attributes required to achieve the Ranger Standard had not changed in over 50 years. However, it seemed from recent student performance, the quality of students' character attributes was what had changed. He then suggested that when the Army's combatant commanders, two-star generals, began sending qualified candidates who could meet the Ranger Standard, graduation rates would once again increase. The senior Army leader looked my commander up and down, agreed that the standard should not change, and agreed to go back and speak to the Army's combatant commanders about sending qualified candidates, not more candidates.

My commander was able to effectively convey the importance of breaking the bell curve of mediocrity and maintain pursuing excellence in the assessment and selection for character attributes necessary for Army Rangers. In the years following, PRCs were reestablished. In 2015, women were successfully integrated into Ranger School, and over 50 women have successfully graduated from the course. I graduated from Ranger School in 1997. I worked there decades later as cadre. The standard of excellence and the test of character have not changed, nor has the character required to become an Army Ranger.

The U.S. Army Ranger School does not care about a candidate's MOS, sex, race, assigned unit, skills, prior experience, or dreams and aspirations. According to the

Ranger Creed, the very ethos of the Ranger Standard, the Ranger School's purpose is to assess, select, train, and transition out to the fighting force "a more elite solider…reliable in battle" with the "intestinal fortitude required to fight on to the Ranger objective and complete the mission though I be the lone survivor" —man or woman.

In today's public and private marketplace, high-performing cultures and cultural leaders will do well to create a culture and ensuing climate in which leaders of character are assessed and selected based upon who can achieve high-performing standards and outcomes.

Breaking the Bell Curve of Mediocrity Requires Overcoming Adversity

No one likes adversity. We don't typically wake up in the morning hoping for more adversity in our lives. Yet the truth is, you are either approaching a time of adversity, in the middle of adversity, or looking back on the most recent adverse event in your life. Adversity assesses our character. Adversity validates or decimates who we are, how we think, and how we lead as people of character. Adversity strengthens or defeats our resolve to continue pursuing a life of excellence. How we resist, respond, and maintain resolve through adversity demonstrates our character.

Character development breaks the bell curve of mediocrity when trusted leaders of character recognize the sacred, foundational essence of calling. Calling is sacred—some would say divine. Character development breaks the bell curve of mediocrity when a trusted leader's character attributes are rooted in an irrevocable calling.

Colonel James "Nick" Rowe, author of the book *Five Years to Freedom*, is credited for developing the U.S. Army's Survival, Evasion, Resistance, and Escape (S.E.R.E.) School attended by high-risk military personnel, including Special Operations and air crews.

His overcoming the adversity of being a prisoner of war for five years during the Vietnam War led him to develop the school to teach personnel how to survive, evade, resist, and escape enemy forces. Col. Rowe's example demonstrates his commitment to what he was called to in life. A calling that overcame adversity and subsequently left a 30-year legacy by training tens of thousands of soldiers how to overcome adversity and remain focused on their calling as warriors, survive, and complete their missions.

We can admit and acknowledge adversity; however, leaders of character refuse to acquiesce to it in our marriages, families, professional careers, community leadership, etc. Becoming overwhelmed by adversity internally or externally occurs when an individual rejects his calling, neglects his giftedness, and fails to adapt to his environment.

For those who have experienced trauma and extreme adversity in life, there may be seasons on this side of the bell curve. However, leaders can either choose to remain there or move forward. For those who remain here, the existential life becomes meaningless. If adversity has overwhelmed you or someone you know in this season of life, please reach out, seek help, and dig deep. Everyone is called to some purpose in life. Every. Single. One of Us.

However, the most dangerous place to find yourself is at society's quintessential peak—the bell curve of mediocrity—where people choose to simply accept adversity and forget their calling.

It sounds like this: "2020 was too hard; it was a wasted year." "COVID has taken advantage of me instead of me taking advantage of COVID." "It is what it is." "It is not worth the effort." "Life is good; what else is there?" "It is a paycheck." "At least we are still together."

Do you know what else is mediocre? Claiming a person is in a constant learning process—always growing and gaining information but failing to actually apply it. Mediocrity, accepting adversity, and forgetting your calling is all about you. Living a life of excellence as a leader of character is about taking ownership of your calling despite adversity and empowering those around you.

So, how do the top 20 percent, the true leaders of character, pursue excellence? They overcome adversity with a laser focus on their calling. They consistently pursue a growth mindset, pursuing excellence-of-character attributes, sharpening talents and giftedness, and embracing whatever environment they find themselves in as an opportunity. They empower those around them to identify their callings, maximize the giftedness of human capital and potential, and shape their environments for excellence.

How have you responded in the past or in a current adverse situation?

How can you respond differently by focusing on your calling?

The Jewish prophet Jeremiah experienced a lifetime of adversity while pursuing his calling as a trusted advisor and leader of character. In the midst of what seemed like overwhelming failure and adversity, he demanded that God give him an answer. God did not provide Jeremiah a direct solution to his problems but rather asked him a question:

> **If you have run with the footmen,**
> **and they have wearied you, then how**
> **can you compete with horses?**
> **(Jeremiah 12:5)**

God's answer to Jeremiah was simple—you must remain focused and committed to your calling to overcome any adversity. We are no different today. To overcome adversity in life, we must remain faithful to pursuing our calling. The bell curve of mediocrity keeps pace with footmen. Leaders of excellence run with the horses.

What adversity are you overcoming today to break the bell curve of mediocrity, validate your character, and use as an opportunity to sharpen your focus on your calling?

If you find yourself *"hard-pressed on every side, yet not crushed; perplexed, but not in despair; persecuted, but not forsaken; struck down, but not destroyed"* *(2 Corinthians 4:8–9)*, then you have an opportunity to break the bell curve of mediocrity and find true joy, fulfillment, and excellence in your sacred calling.

BREAKING THE BELL CURVE OF MEDIOCRITY REQUIRES A PRACTICE OF DISCIPLINED OBEDIENCE

WE ARE A fighting family. I've studied martial arts for over 30 years. My daughter, a senior, is in her fourth season on the high school varsity wrestling team. She was the first female to join the team and the first female to wrestle in the state championships, and she finished with a 5-2 record, placing seventh out of 50 girls in her weight class. Now as a senior, she is the first female team captain. She teaches kids jujitsu at her BJJ school as a blue belt. Both of our sons train and compete in jujitsu, judo, and wrestling.

We often discuss how disciplined obedience breaks the bell curve of mediocrity as young adults living in a world full of distractions and denial. What does that look like practically? Family time, not Facebook time. Identity in virtue, not image by Instagram. Exercise versus excess. Faith over fear. Anchored, not anxious.

Many times we've discussed the ancient parable of the sower, seed, and fields, as found in many philosophical and religious traditions. To keep it simple:

Tilling the soil is the hard routine.
Spreading the seed is the meticulous routine.
Watering the seed is the continuous routine.
Harvesting the crop is the rewarding routine.
Leaders of character practice disciplined obedience.

The bell curve of mediocrity is dominated by diversionary distractions and anchored by dilemma-draining denial.

The character development of disciplined obedience breaks the bell curve of mediocrity by embracing the mindset of hard, meticulous, continuous, and rewarding routines.

In ancient Hebrew, the word for obedience is *shema*. It means to listen and hear. In Hebrew, it means to obey. I find that interesting. In some of the most ancient wisdom literature in the world, obedience means to listen. Listening means to obey. When leaders of character pursue disciplined listening, they break the bell curve of mediocrity by avoiding distractions and dilemmas through obedience and spend more time listening to wisdom.

An unbelieving heart and mind refuse to listen to or obey some character-defining discipline or ethos. They self-medicate on denial and distraction to avoid obedience. Instead of practicing permanence, they are consumed with emotive experience.

People who deny or outright reject a greater disciplined obedience, ethos, or objective truth to shape their character find themselves in a constant dilemma of their own myopic reality. It typically sounds like this, "Hard work is relative, attention to detail is controlling, and continuity is boring, but I deserve a reward like everyone else." Refusing to listen to truth, they find themselves in constant dilemmas through denial.

People who live an inch away from a greater disciplined obedience, ethos, or objective truth and know it to be true yet refuse to accept or follow such an ethos will experience the medio-crity of diversion through distraction. It typically sounds like this, "I know. Yeah, I know. I know. I know." They know the hard, meticulous, continuous, and rewarding routine, but they choose an array of distractions to divert them from what they know to be true. The bell curve of mediocrity acknowledges what disciplined obedience is and rejects it by offering diversion through distraction such as the glorified pursuit of sophisticated moral ambiguity over truth.

When leaders of character internalize disciplined obedience and embrace the hard, meticulous, continuous, and rewarding routines, they empower organizational cultures and enable climates that pursue excellence. When culture is built on leaders of character who exercise disciplined obedience, culture will absolutely eat strategy for lunch. In the military, the warrior ethos is driven by the self-regulating warrior's code which is adhered to and regulated by warriors with character through disciplined obedience. In sports, a disciplined obedience includes a team mindset such as "winning the N.O.W. (no opportunity wasted)." High-performing cultures recruit, develop, and operationalize leaders of character who excel in disciplined obedience.

Disciplined obedience is a continual exercise of character development, listening and obeying a character-shaping code, ethos, and practice. Committing to hard, meticulous, and continuous routines may at times seem fruitless in seasons of tilling, sowing, and watering when the results have not yet presented themselves. However, as leaders of character will discover and affirm, breaking the bell curve of mediocrity through disciplined obedience is worth the reward.

How do people of faith break the bell curve of mediocrity? We exercise the disciplined obedience required to live a more excellent life in community with one another as we prioritize worshipping, obeying, and listening to God. The *Shema* and the Apostles' Creed are two ancient examples of spiritually disciplined obedience. They develop our character, empowering us to live a more excellent life full of practice, passion, purpose, and precision.

Read the *Shema* in Deuteronomy 6:1–12, specifically verses 4–9. This is a traditional Jewish prayer reinforcing disciplined obedience:

> Hear, O Israel: The Lord our God, the Lord is one. Love the Lord your God with all your heart and with all your soul and with all your strength. These commandments that I give you today are to be on your hearts. Impress them on your children. Talk about them when you sit at home and when you walk along the road, when you lie down and when you get up. Tie them as symbols on your hands and bind them on your foreheads. Write them on the doorframes of your houses and on your gates.

Read the Apostles' Creed. It was established by 380 A.D. from the Nicene Creed of 325 A.D. The creed unites Christians across the world in pursuing a disciplined obedience to affirming non-negotiable tenets of their faith:

> I believe in God, the Father almighty, Creator of heaven and earth, and in Jesus Christ, his only Son, our Lord, who was conceived by the Holy Spirit, born of the Virgin Mary, suffered under Pontius Pilate, was crucified, died and was buried; he descended into hell; on the third day he rose again from the dead; he ascended into heaven, and is seated at the right hand of God the Father almighty; from there he will come to judge the living and the dead. I believe in the Holy Spirit, the holy catholic Church, the communion of saints, the forgiveness of sins, the resurrection of the body, and life everlasting. Amen.

To be a leader of character who practices a life of disciplined obedience, one must be a disciple of someone he listens to. Who are you listening to?

BREAKING THE BELL CURVE OF MEDIOCRITY WITH ACTIVE FAITH AND ROBUST CHARACTER

LET US REVIEW the three previous perspectives regarding how character development breaks the bell curve of mediocrity. First, excelling through character separates us from accepting mediocrity and ultimately from selecting out. Second, when we act on faith, our calling steadies us in overcoming adversity. However, accepting adversity results from forgetting our calling or rejecting our calling when overwhelmed by internal or external adversity. Third, living a life of disciplined obedience separates us from the mediocrity of diversionary distractions and succumbing to dilemmas when, out of a lack of character, we live in denial. So, let's wrap up with this—*Life is an obstacle course requiring an active faith and robust character.*

When teaching character development, I use a challenging obstacle course, built according to the specifications of varying Special Operations obstacle courses. The course is challenging in and of itself. Participants normally run through the course one time, navigating 12 obstacles that test core strength, agility, speed, and self-confidence. Balance beams, monkey bars, vertical and horizontal ropes, climbing walls, and vertical and horizontal obstacles require finesse, strength, and technique. Elite athletes can complete it under 10 minutes. I've seen Rangers from the 75th Ranger Regiment do it in seven minutes, but the average time is closer to 20 minutes. We make it harder.

We begin with three rounds of five pullups, 10 pushups, and 15 air squats. Participants are given 20 minutes and penalized with burpees for breaking time. For any obstacle an individual cannot navigate after three attempts, he must do another 10 burpees. Once someone completes the course, he navigates four obstacles again.

The balance beam is done with a 35-pound backpack while carrying a 35-pound kettlebell in one hand and memorizing facts to a narrated story. Next, they must navigate the monkey bars while simultaneously memorizing up to 15 images being displayed on a flip chart, one at a time every two to three seconds. Then, they must navigate four 6-foot walls as teams for three iterations, completing each iteration in less time, again punishable by burpees. Then they climb a 30-foot rope while listening to a list of words they must write down upon descending the rope. Finally, they conduct a 5–7-minute mindfulness exercise, focusing on breath control, centeredness, and relaxation.

What is the purpose? To demonstrate that character breaks the bell curve of mediocrity. Life is an obstacle course. How we assess, navigate, and complete life's obstacles reveals character virtues that define us. When physical, mental, and emotional strain occurs through pressure, duress, and time, one's true character is revealed.

Breaking the bell curve of mediocrity requires character traits and virtues that acknowledge obstacles exist, assess the situation, endure the navigation, and learn from reflection on the experience. Breaking the bell curve of mediocrity requires a mindset that knows we are always facing an obstacle, navigating an obstacle, or learning from past experience to excel in the next opportunity.

Renowned Yale Professor Miroslav Volf writes in *A Public Faith*, when discussing the key to human flourishing, "Virtuous character matters more than moral knowledge…faith idles when character shrivels."[7] Human flourishing doesn't settle for mediocrity; it seeks a life well lived.

So, how does practicing permanence in character development break the bell curve of mediocrity?

> ***Character:*** *Dominates circumstances versus being devoured by circumstances.*

*Character: Prepares for victory
versus being dominated by defeat.*

*Character: Pursues the virtue of wisdom
versus the vices of arrogance and foolishness.*

*Character: Trains, resists, suffers, perfects,
establishes, strengthens, and excels.*

*An active faith and robust character reject
idle faith and shriveled character.*

Consider these 11 mediocrity-breaking questions as you assess your character and passionate, purposeful, and precise pursuit of living a life of excellence.

- How did you take advantage of COVID?

- What character attributes empowered you to overcome and excel over COVID's obstacles?

- Where did you fail forward over the past year?

- Where is your hope, especially when obstacles overcame you this year?

- Who will assess, navigate, and overcome the obstacles of life with you?

- How did an active faith and robust character elevate, empower, expand, and encourage others?

- What mental, emotional, spiritual, physical, and relational steps can you take to move forward?

- What self-limiting beliefs do you need to reject, and what character attributes can you accept?

- What awareness do you have now regarding living a life of character that you did not have before?

- In the next year, how will your character assess, navigate, and overcome obstacles?

- What makes evaluating an active faith and robust character significant for you?

3

TRAIN YOUR TRUST AND TRUST YOUR TRAINING

The Hard Routine

–British SAS

THE BRITISH SAS, the United Kingdom's elite counterterrorism unit, uses the term "hard routine" to describe their mindset when going on a mission. Andy McNab describes this process in his book, *Bravo Two Zero*. The moment they step off on a mission, their intent, mindset, and actions are passionate, purposeful, and precise. "There is no room for selfishness, indulgence, compromise, or distraction"[8] on such missions.

They trust their character. They trust the fidelity of their training process. And they entrust their lives to one another.

TRAINING YOUR TRUST IS A SOUL ISSUE

TRAINING YOUR TRUST requires knowing who you are as a person of character. Intrinsically, what passionate calling drives you? What purposeful virtues guide you? How does precision focus you? The hard routine is more than a mindset for a mission—it's a lifestyle of permanence. It's trusting who you are, how you think, and what you do.

If training our trust begins with an understanding of our character, it is helpful to consider the makeup of our character. I believe we are all created in the image of God, the *Imago Dei*. That means we have a fixed point of trust in someone or something bigger than ourselves. The Stoics referred to this essence as the *Logos*. In the Judeo-Christian tradition, it is God who displays incommunicable and communicable attributes.

How do the character attributes of God train our trust? Theologians differentiate God's attributes by placing them into two categories. Incommunicable attributes are traits possessed only by God and not shared with anyone else. Communicable attributes are traits God shares with His creation.

Three major incommunicable traits are omnipotence, omnipresence, and omniscience—in other words, an all-powerful, all-knowing, and all-present God. There is no military might, political power, academic institution, or technological advancement that can compare. We attempt to use finite resources to control what we cannot control, attempting to replace the incommunicable character of God. Training our trust in God is essential since we lack the power, wisdom, and presence to control every situation.

From Plato to Aquinas, philosophers have identified God's communicable attributes. We find God's communicable attributes, such as justice, wisdom, love, and temperance, across cultures and belief systems. They are necessary to lead ourselves, people, and teams.

However, even though we pursue the rule of law and a just authority, we fall short of God's law and need His redemptive grace. We can pursue wisdom, knowledge, and understanding and remain confused by some of humanity's greatest questions. We can love to the fullest and yet hurt those we love the most, falling short of loving unconditionally. We desire God's mercy and yet struggle with extending temperance and mercy in our own decisions.

Training to trust God for things we cannot control and for character growth in the things we can is a spiritual discipline. Scripture, prayers, songs, journaling, and meditation are effective disciplines to train our trust in God. You may be asking at this point, "What about people who do not believe in God?" Great question! I believe everyone believes in a "big G" God or "little g" god. We either train our trust in a big God or believe we are god. Here is something to consider—if you believe you are the god of your life, would you or others want to trust, obey, and worship you, or would you be looking for a God who is a little more all-knowing, all-powerful, and all-present?

Toward the end of a deployment, one of our special operators joined me at a table in our dining facility. "My times are in your hands," he stated with a stoic voice. I looked up from my meal and smiled. "My times are in your hands," he stated again. I verbally affirmed hearing him this time, acknowledging his reference to Psalm 31:15, "My times are in Your hand; deliver me from the hand of my enemies, and from those who persecute me."

He wasn't a regular chapel attendee. However, on one occasion when he did attend, this was the message I shared with the audience. I asked him what this verse meant to him at the end of this deployment since his mission required him to work remotely in hostile environments, many times alone or with a small team. He told me this became his prayer every time he left the security of our compound. His assured confidence in or reliance on the character of God was an act of faith in training his trust in God's communicable and incommunicable qualities.

He lessened fear. He enhanced faith.

He trained his trust in the things he could control.

He put trust in God for what he could not control.

He trusted his training amid a VUCA environment and accomplished his mission, not just once but hundreds of times.

TRAINING YOUR TRUST IS A MINDSET

WE MUST ALSO train our trust in how we make decisions. Remember Aristotle's quote from Chapter 1? It is not easy to approach the mean of excellence, nor is it for everyone. Implementing spiritual disciplines and virtuous intent requires the environment in which to practice them. Samuel Wells writes in his book *Improvisation*, "The moral life should not be experienced as an agony of impossible choice. Instead, it should be a matter of habit and instinct. Learning to live well is about gaining the right habits and instincts, rather than making the right choices."[9] Habits and instincts have more influence on our decision-making processes than logic and reason.

Dan Kahneman, Pulitzer Prize-winning author of *Thinking Fast and Slow*, argues that we make 98 percent of our decisions with our System 1, or our amygdala, where we receive our fight-or-flight responses for survival. Kahneman notes this is where we find "cognitive ease." System 2, our prefrontal cortex where we make two percent of our decisions using logic and reason, requires additional "cognitive strain." [10] The only Mr. Spock to exist was the one in the television show *Star Trek*. No individual makes completely rational, logical decisions void of emotion.

Training our decision-making process is more than what some may reference as muscle memory or sets and reps. Our character impacts our decision-making process which in turn requires memory recall or intuition. Training our trust in environments where we can practice decision making and then review, adapt, and overcome is critical.

Two physicians were discussing such revelations of practice when one of their fellow physicians tragically lost a child on the operating table due to unexpected complications. One physician expressed leniency and empathy for the surgeon, imagining the difficulty of handling a crisis in surgery. The other colleague expressed the opposite, saying:

I think the man is to blame. If anybody had handed me ether instead of chloroform, I would have known from the weight it was the wrong thing. You see, I know the man well. We were students together at Aberdeen and he could have become one of the finest surgeons in Europe if only he had given his mind to it. But he didn't. He was more interested in golf. So, he just used to do enough work to pass his examinations and no more. And that is how he has lived his life—just enough to get through, but no more; so, he has never picked up those seemingly peripheral bits of knowledge that can one day be crucial. The other day in that theater a bit of "peripheral" knowledge was crucial and he didn't have it. But it wasn't the other day that he failed—it was thirty-nine years ago, when he only gave himself half-heartedly to medicine.[11]

Herein lies the tension between practice and experience. Résumés, social media postings, and professional bios all claim a certain number of years of experience, not practice. However, listen to the narrative of professions whose practice has permanence. Lawyers practice law. Doctors practice medicine. Soldiers practice war. Experience can be deceiving. However, one's practice reveals the true professional. There are written and unwritten rules about professions, specified and implied tasks, and central and peripheral knowledge. True professionals train to trust their decision-making processes long before the day they must make professional decisions.

When making moral and ethical decisions, we spend time looking at our psychological and moral development and how that impacts our decision-making process. In short, training to trust our process requires having a process and practicing it regularly.

First, we need to identify the pain point, problem, or

situation at hand. We need to ask ourselves if this is a manageable tension or if we must solve the problem quickly. Tension isn't necessarily a bad thing. Leaders of character in high-performing organizations know when to manage tensions and when to solve a problem. It may also be wiser to solve a problem with 80 percent of the information now rather than waiting for a 100 percent solution that comes too late.

Second, we need to evaluate what options are available. How do those options align or fragment our personal morals and virtues and our organizational ethics or rules, and are we willing to live with the good or potentially bad consequences?

Third, we must commit to a decision, trusting our training, and trusting the advice, expertise, and training of trusted advisors.

Fourth, we need to act. At times, our environment provides space to consider the process. At other times, it is a split-second decision, and our habits and instincts will take over.

TRAINING YOUR TRUST REQUIRES "THIS MUCH"

WHEN PEOPLE HEAR "train your trust, trust your training, and commit to the hard routine," many of us may default to thinking of exercise and athletic training. Some would say that on the athletic field or in military training, leadership is 90 percent physical and 10 percent athletic. Ted Williams, the only Major League player to ever finish a season hitting over .400, said that hitting a baseball was the hardest thing to do in any single sport.

When we observe professional athletes, we must re-member the thousands of hours of continuous training they completed to effectively compete at such high levels. At times, the "grind" is boring and monotonous. Concepts such as "the grind," "hard routine," and "trusting the process" require discipline, physical, mental, and emotional stamina, and endurance.

Physically training your trust is more than what some may call muscle memory or completing 10,000 repetitions. It's ensuring your training regimen records the correct memory of each movement or exercise and that there is a precise approach to each of the 10,000 repetitions.

What is the difference between leaders of excellence and those who pursue mediocrity? "This much." When you read "this much," I want you to hold up your thumb and index finger an inch from one another as if prepared to pinch something. That's the difference. "This much." It's not a lot. It's a little, every single day, consistently, for a lifetime. Leaders who seek perfection in their practice commit to a process of "this much" because *their practice is their profession*. This is what separates mediocrity from excellence—"this much."

What does that look like? Dry firing your firearm 500 times before ever putting a round in the chamber. Composing a song and then practicing it in small segments incrementally until they are perfect before ever playing the entire song. Breaking down a film before the team arrives. Mentally running every play in your head in a relaxed state of meditation before ever stepping onto the field of play. Conducting candid and honest reviews of a performance after an event.

Training your trust is the process of living the hard routine of "this much" every day, more than everyone else. How well we train our trust impacts how we will trust our training at decisive points in life.

Trust Your Training

I'VE HAD THE privilege of serving in combat with some of the most elite Special Operations forces in the world. Trusting their training is second nature. It's automatic. It's natural. It's a lifetime of the hard routine. It's the life story and legacy of Larry Boivin.

The White Mountains of New Hampshire provided the ultimate training environment for a future professional soldier to learn to trust his identity, instinct, and action. As a young man, Larry and his brothers spent countless hours in the mountains playing war games.

Larry was a warrior, statesman, leader, and innovator. He was a professional who could transform from a blood-and-sweat-covered warrior to suit-and-tie executive, always with the same easygoing smile and introduction, "Hey, how's it goin'? I'm Larry Boivin."

I first met Larry in the summer of 1998 when I returned from an overseas deployment. Walking into our company headquarters, I ran into a quiet and humble warrior with his arms folded across his chest and his back and one foot resting up against the wall. It looked as if he had just finished working out—knowing Larry, it was probably for the second or third time that day. I can only describe him as an inverted triangle on top of a rectangular block with dark curly hair and a large mustache, sweating through a brown t-shirt and black running shorts. He was an imposing figure.

I introduced myself, and he told me he was my new platoon sergeant. I would come to learn he was the best platoon sergeant a young officer could ever desire. He taught me the hard routine. He taught me to train my trust and trust my training. He taught me what it meant to be a professional. He taught me "this much" more every day. Larry and I would have the opportunity to serve together again in different support roles in a Special Operations unit several years later. We became lifelong friends.

Larry epitomized the warrior ethos. He began as an Army cook and went on to become an Army Ranger. Then, he pursued a unique career. He was specially assessed and selected to serve in an Army Special Operations Unit in a new role as a "master breacher"— basically, a demolitions expert who could go anywhere, anytime, and provide incredibly effective results. Larry liked to blow things up at a Ph.D. level. Those who served with him will affirm his tenacity, loyalty, and courage under fire. There is no doubt he set the standard for the next generation that followed as one of the first Special Operations master breachers.

He was awarded the Silver Star, an award subordinate only to the Distinguished Service Cross and Medal of Honor. He was also awarded the Purple Heart for his actions on April 26, 2004, in Iraq. His citation reads,

> While providing training and support to a small Marine contingency, Sergeant Major Boivin's unit was attacked from several locations by a large massing enemy force. During the first minutes of the attack, 50 percent of the Marine forces were incapacitated. During the initial attack, RPG [rocket propelled grenades] were impacting all around him and he was hit by shrapnel from an RPG round in close prox-

imity to his location. During the attack he withstood several penetrating wounds to the left side of the head, legs, and buttock. After regaining composure, he fought back with the remaining Marines until wounded again by a fragmentation grenade. Later, with a comrade, he provided covering support to allow the Marines to evacuate the wounded. Once all the wounded Marines were safe or moving back to a safe location, Sergeant Major Boivin and his teammate bounded back toward the Marine Forward Operating Base (FOB) while continuing to provide covering fire for our Marines until the rest made it back to safety.

A picture is worth a thousand words. A photo, framed with his award, captures Larry on one knee with blood dripping off his t-shirt, fully exposed on a rooftop while returning deadly effective fire on enemy forces.

The love and protective spirit he had for his brothers

resonates in the stories they tell of their childhood antics as the "White Mountain Boys." He was a loyal son to his mother and father. As one of his family members says, "Larry was the Godfather." He was a quiet man of faith—a faith that was practiced daily, forged in combat, and permanent in life.

LIVING THE HARD ROUTINE

LARRY TRAINED HIS trust and trusted his training, living a life of excellence. He committed to the hard routine every day. On November 15, 2012, Larry and his wife were riding on a parade float honoring veterans and their spouses. Several factors contributed to what happened next. As the flatbed parade float crossed the railroad tracks, it paused due to the floats ahead of it. An oncoming freight train bore down at a high rate of speed.

Larry's last living act was throwing his wife, Angela, off the float and out of danger before final impact. There was no debate, no deliberation, no discussion. Trained trust, trusted training. My heart broke when Angela called me. I was humbled and honored to preside over Larry's funeral and burial in Arlington National Cemetery. I remember to give "this much" every day in honor of my friend Larry.

Larry once gave me a bottle of bourbon for a promotion, and we enjoyed it together. The case it came in sits on my desk today with his photo inside. Wearing his dress uniform on his retirement day, the picture reveals him holding his grandson's hand and having a talk with the young man when he was a child. Fifteen years later, Angela brought me another bottle of bourbon for my retirement from the Army, but that one will remain sealed.

One of the families seated next to Larry and Angie in the parade was Sergeant Major (USA, retired) William Lubbers and his wife, Tiffanie. The outcome was the same. Willie's last full measure of devotion was pushing Tiffanie to safety. Witnesses recall seeing people remaining on the flatbed truck pushing others to safety as the flatbed trailer took the full brunt force of the train. There is no doubt they saw Larry and Willie.

I had the privilege of serving in the same Special Forces unit as Willie. Like Larry, Willie served multiple tours of combat in Afghanistan and Iraq and was awarded the Purple Heart and three Bronze Stars. Willie was a beloved leader in the Special Forces community, and he trained the trust and trusted the training of those he led and served. Several years later, while teaching a course on transformational moral leadership to Army officer candidates, I noticed the nametag of a young officer candidate—"Lubbers." Despite past trauma, present opportunities, and inevitable future risk, Willie's son chose to pursue the hard routine like his father, becoming an Army Ranger and infantry officer. He continues to serve in the Army today, and like his father, trains his trust and trusts his training.

4

SHOW UP. PLAY UP. FINISH.

"Not For The Weak or Fainthearted."

–Sign Outside U.S. Army Ranger School

SHOW UP

IN 1991, AN Army recruiter came to my house and gave me a "Be All You Can Be" trifold brochure. Upon opening, it displayed three pictures with a clear heading above each photo: "AIRBORNE," "RANGER," "SPECIAL FORCES." The pictures were of men jumping out of airplanes and crawling through swamps, armed to the teeth and being all they could be. I asked him if I could sign up for all of those opportunities, and he said, "No."

Instead, I applied to attend the United States Military Academy at West Point. Their promotional poster, which I still have today, says, "Much of the history we teach was made by the people we taught." Unfortunately, my SAT scores were subpar. In fact, I never scored above 1000 collectively on the combined math and verbal. My ACT scores were average.

When the area representative admissions officer explained to my parents and me that I was not qualified to even be considered to attend West Point, I asked him for a 30-minute interview. After the interview, he had a different perspective. He left my application file open because of the intangibles he observed that test scores do not measure. They do not measure the character attributes necessary to show up, play up, and finish.

On the last day a candidate could find out about attending West Point, I received a phone call from my congressman to inform me that I was a third alternate for an appointment and the first two candidates had turned their appointments down. I told the congressman I had already accepted a four-year ROTC scholarship to Boston University, and my dad slapped the phone out of my hand and asked me what I was thinking! I picked the phone back up, accepted the appointment, and headed to West Point.

I barely scratched out a 2.0 GPA my freshman year, including a D in chemistry. I failed English composition my junior year and had to take it twice. However, I graduated on the Dean's List the last three semesters with a 3.0 GPA, earned a black belt in Japanese jujitsu, and won a national championship in four-wall handball. I was commissioned as a second lieutenant with my classmates.

During my senior year, my roommate and I both aspired to become Army Rangers. We hung a large black-and-gold ranger tab on the back of our door with a map of the Balkans and the quote, "Somewhere, someone is training to kill you today. What are you doing about it?"

We developed a training regimen that would prepare us for a life-changing experience a year later. He went on to become a very successful Green Beret Special Forces Officer and was awarded a Purple Heart and Bronze Star in combat.

I showed up January 2, 1997, with U.S. Army Ranger School Class 3-97, not knowing what to expect. I only knew I had been practicing for this day for several years. Ranger School is 62 days for a small percentage of students who make it "straight through." However, the majority of students "recycle" at least one of the three phases, meaning they have to do the entire phase all over again. I spent 120 days in Ranger School with my entire platoon being recycled together in the Florida "Swamp Phase." Our entire platoon except for one graduated together on our second attempt.

Ranger School, like other elite military training schools, is not for the weak or fainthearted, especially when you must overcome adversity, push through injuries, and build relationships under duress. Life circumstances are no different. The first step is showing up. The next step is playing up. Finally, finish what you started. Regardless of circumstances, naysayers, odds, or your own self-esteem, keep showing up.

What is required to show up? It requires the virtue of courage—the courage to act when fear and trepidation try to take hold and the courage to act with self-control and not bravado or recklessness at the expense of others or causing burnout to yourself. Showing up requires courage to faithfully trust in your calling, seek growth in your gifts and abilities, and boldly embrace new environments, leaving behind the comfort of what is known.

To show up, you must learn to control the controllable, embrace the suck, and get comfortable being uncomfortable. When you show up, you focus on what is present now. You acknowledge that the road less traveled is difficult, adversity is normal, and the obstacle is the way. You embrace a growth mindset and new people, places, and processes. How do you practice showing up permanently? *Show up where you know you are called to be every single day.*

Play Up

"Act like you've been there before" is a familiar phrase referenced by football coaches and players on how to act after scoring a touchdown in the end zone. In the military, we often remind people, "Do your job." In Special Operations, it is common to hear that quiet professionals simply bring their "A game" every day.

It was a humble privilege and honor to serve the people who make up elite organizations such as Special Operations units and Major League Baseball. What I discovered is a group of amazing people full of character and talent who practice more than anyone else so that when it is time to play, they play with excellence—what they practiced became permanent.

Showing up and playing up is not optional—it's required. Even more so, it is desired by those in such professions. We look for it in the assessment and selection process. We grow it in the training and development process. We promote it in the retention process. What is the thread of continuity throughout these steps of the talent management process? Character.

Organizations that hire people of character who play up and create a culture where playing up is normal and expected every day achieve excellence. These organizations create climates where autonomy is earned, freedom is exercised, and excellence is constantly pursued through practice.

Research studying how Special Operations assess and select their personnel identifies that playing up requires a greater capacity of character than skills or talent. We know for a fact that when people are put under duress emotionally, mentally, and physically, their true character comes out. Playing up requires character attributes such as integrity, courage, perseverance, personal responsibility, professionalism, adaptability, being a team player, and capability.[12] No surprise that many of these traits are required for showing up, and without a doubt, they are necessary to finish. How do your character attributes compare to the ones mentioned here? How do they empower you to play up?

FINISH

PROFESSIONALS WHO PRACTICE well finish well. They leave a permanence of who they are, what they do, and who they impact.

In 8th grade, I experienced two God shaping events highlighting the importance of showing up, playing up, and finishing. I was named our junior high school basketball team's Best Defensive Player, but not because I was a good basketball player. The words my coach expressed to the entire team were this. He told us no one plays with more tenacity. He did not mention rebounds, blocking shots, or blocking players out of the paint. He mentioned character. I had tenacity. Coach Woody probably does not realize the character-shaping event that took place that night when he labeled me as a tenacious person of character. It would soon be tested.

Later that spring, I was asked to run America's All-Time Best 10K race, The Bolder Boulder, with a young woman I was infatuated with. At fourteen years old, you do some pretty crazy things for love. I trained for three months to run the race because I was not a natural runner. I was a baseball player. I ran ninety feet at a time. My friends called me up two days before the race and invited me to do something different that weekend, so insignificant, I cannot even remember what we did. What I do clearly remember is life's distractions kept me from my goal. I no-showed the girl. I never ran the race.

Yet, two weeks later, I received a letter in the mail from the Bolder Boulder congratulating me for finishing the race! Enclosed, at the bottom of the congratulatory note, was a polaroid picture of my "photo finish." But the picture was not of me. The picture was of a man, wearing my bib number and crossing the finish line with his hands raised in the air. At fourteen years old, on that day I made a commitment, I would never let anyone else ever run a race I was called to run. It was time to exercise tenacity and commit to a lifetime of practice. Almost thirty-five years later, that story still resonates with me as I'm faithfully running the race God called me to run. What is the difference? Practicing permanence. "This much" every day. Showing up, playing up, and finishing.

Leaders who finish well have a firm foundation in their faith and identity in who they are created to be. Second, they surround themselves with other trusted professionals who provide coaching, mentoring, and wise counsel. Third, their leadership influence develops more leaders, not more followers. Leaders of character who finish well know practice makes permanent, so they ensure what they practice is passionate, purposeful, and precise. Show Up. Play Up. Finish.

ENDNOTES

1   Shelton, Josephus, *A History of the Jewish War*, 3.71–97, n.d.

2 "Masutatsu Oyama," n.d., https://www.masutatsuoyama.com/philosophical_thoughts.htm.

3   Geoffrey Scarre, *On Courage, Thinking in Action* (New York: Routledge, 2010)

4   Richie Norton, *The Power of Something Stupid* (Salt Lake City: Shadow Mountain, 2013).

5   H.R. McMaster, *Battlegrounds: The Fight to Defend the Free World, First Edition* (New York: Harper Collins, 2020), 158.

6   Aristotle, *Nicomachean Ethics* (Oxford: Oxford University Press, 2009).

[7] Miroslav Volf, *A Public Faith: How Followers of Christ Should Serve the Common Good* (Grand Rapids, Michigan: Brazos Press, 2011), 13.

[8] Jason Dougherty, "The Hard Routine," *CrossFit Journal* 69 (May 2008).

[9] Samuel Wells, *Improvisation: The Drama of Christian Ethics* (Grand Rapids, Michigan: Brazos Press, 2004), 75.

[10] Daniel Kahneman, *Thinking Fast and Slow* (New York: Farrar, Strauss, and Giroux, 2011), 59.

[11] Donald Nicholl, *Holiness* (London: Darton, Longman & Todd, 1981), 54–55.

[12] Mike Sarraille, George Randle, and Josh Cotton, *The Talent War* (Lioncrest Publishing, 2020), 107.

CPSIA information can be obtained
at www.ICGtesting.com
Printed in the USA
JSHW052129160222
22955JS00005B/18

9 781956 267365